S

DANGEROUS DRUGS

AMPHETAMINES

GERRY BOEHME

Cavendish
Square

New York

Published in 2016 by Cavendish Square Publishing, LLC
243 5th Avenue, Suite 136, New York, NY 10016

Library of Congress Cataloging-in-Publication Data

Boehme, Gerry, author.
Amphetamines / Gerry Boehme.
pages cm. — (Dangerous drugs)
Includes bibliographical references and index.
ISBN 978-1-50260-560-3 (hardcover) ISBN 978-1-50260-561-0 (ebook)
1. Amphetamines—Juvenile literature. 2. Amphetamine abuse—Juvenile literature. I. Title.

RC568.A45B64 2016
613.8'4—dc23

2015007583

Editorial Director: David McNamara
Editor: Fletcher Doyle
Copy Editor: Rebecca Rohan
Art Director: Jeff Talbot
Designer: Stephanie Flecha
Senior Production Manager: Jennifer Ryder-Talbot
Production Editor: Renni Johnson
Photo Research: J8 Media

The photographs in this book are used by permission and through the courtesy of: Science Source/Getty Images, cover and 1; Frederic J. Brown/AFP/Getty Images, 4; Nu-Creation/iStockphoto.com, 7; Terry Vine/Getty Images, 10; Terry J/iStockphoto.com, 13; Tasos Katopodis/Getty Images, 17; MGM Studios/Moviepix/Getty Images, 19; Meletios/Shutterstock.com, 21; Lisa Peardon/The Image Bank/Getty Images, 23; Simone van den Berg/Shutterstock.com, 24; Badahos/Shutterstock.com, 27; Muammer Mujdat Uzel/Getty Images, 28; Keizer PD/Splash News/Newscom, 32; AP Photo/Patrick Semansky, 37; Hulton Archive/Getty Images, 39; Byllwill/Getty Images, 41; Sahachat Saneha/Shutterstock.com, 42; Trista Weibell/Getty Images, 45; Maga/Shutterstock.com, 48; Brendan Hoffman/Getty Images, 51; Maica/istockphoto.com, 52; aldomurillo/iStockphoto.com, 56.

Printed in the United States of America

Contents

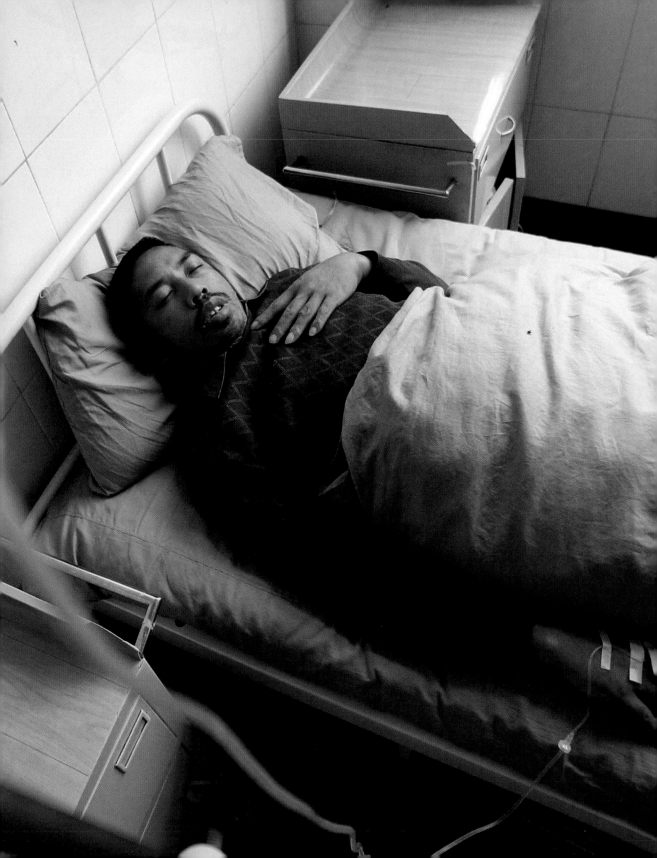

CHAPTER ONE

Wrong Path

WOULDN'T IT BE GREAT IF YOU COULD DO something to help you concentrate better in school, have more energy, and feel more alert?

In 2012, the *New York Times* published a story about a recent graduate from McLean High School in Virginia, one of the top public schools in the Washington, DC, area.

Late in his sophomore year, the boy wanted some help to raise his B average. He began taking a **drug** called Adderall, and it seemed to increase his concentration. At first he took 10 milligrams of the drug per day, but as the effects wore off he started taking more and more. Within a year he was up to 300 milligrams a day.

One night, after he had taken about 400 milligrams, his heart started beating wildly. He began hallucinating and

Amphetamine abuse can cause serious medical problems and even death.

then convulsing. He was rushed to the emergency room and wound up spending seven months at a drug treatment center. To his surprise, two other patients at the center were also being treated for abusing **stimulants** in high school.

People are always looking for ways to feel better, be more successful, and be more popular. To do that, we should first try to change our own behavior to improve our situation. For instance, we can get more sleep so we don't feel tired. We can train harder to improve our performance at sports. We can eat healthy foods to increase our energy or lose weight.

Sometimes, however, we might need a doctor's help to get well, and as part of the treatment the doctor might **prescribe** medicine to help cure us. On the other hand, people who aren't sick and don't need medicine can still be tempted to use drugs incorrectly, believing that these substances can make their lives better.

Amphetamines are one type of drug that can provide a lot of help to those in need but can also be abused, especially by students. Amphetamines are stimulant drugs—they increase alertness and physical activity by stimulating the central nervous system, including the brain.

Unfortunately, misusing these powerful drugs can cause serious problems. People who abuse amphetamines can ruin their own health and hurt their relationships with family and friends. Society also pays a price, since drug abuse leads to more crime and higher costs for treatment and prevention programs.

Stimulants Are Everywhere

Many people start their day with a cup of coffee. It's a part of their regular routine, as natural as waking up, rising out of bed, and getting dressed. Coffee drinkers believe that their morning cup helps make them more alert and gets them ready to face the challenges of the day ahead.

Some teens may not realize that coffee contains caffeine, a strong stimulant drug.

The boost in energy that people feel when they drink coffee comes from caffeine, a common stimulant. Caffeine occurs naturally in coffee and tea but can also be found in many soft drinks, energy drinks, and other foods.

While caffeine can help us stay alert, too much can cause anxiety, headaches, and "the jitters" (nervousness). Caffeine is also **addictive**, and a person who suddenly stops drinking coffee may experience **withdrawal** symptoms.

There are many different types of stimulant drugs. While these substances can be used to treat many conditions, they can differ from each other in important ways, and some people may respond better to one drug than another. Some of these drugs can be much more powerful than caffeine, and therefore even more dangerous. Amphetamines fit this description.

The name "amphetamines" actually refers to a family of substances that all have similar effects on the body. Amphetamines are known by many names. Examples of prescribed amphetamines include Adderall, Benzedrine, Dexedrine, Dextrostat, Desoxyn, ProCentra, and Vyvanse. Amphetamines are also sometimes referred to as bennies, speed, and uppers, especially by those who use them without a prescription.

The drug Adderall is based on amphetamines and is used by many doctors to treat a disease called Attention Deficit Hyperactivity Disorder (**ADHD**). Children with ADHD have significant difficulty paying attention, sitting still,

waiting their turn, or concentrating for extended periods of time. Experts think that ADHD is caused when someone's brain doesn't produce enough of the chemicals it needs to help them pay attention and control their impulses. Doctors prescribe Adderall to help children perform more effectively at school and behave better at home.

Amphetamines are also commonly prescribed to treat conditions like narcolepsy and obesity. People with narcolepsy have an uncontrollable urge to sleep. People who are extremely overweight may have trouble controlling their appetite. Proper use of amphetamines can help these people live normal lives.

A Long History

Amphetamines are based on a chemical called ephedrine, a natural substance found in the ma huang plant (*Ephedra vulgaris*). The Chinese have used this plant for centuries to treat asthma.

In 1887, chemists first made amphetamine as a **synthetic** substitute for ephedrine. They found that amphetamine affected the brain by increasing alertness and decreasing appetite. Amphetamine use began to skyrocket in the 1920s when chemist Gordon A. Alles changed the formula so doctors could better treat asthma, hay fever, and colds. In 1932, Smith Kline & French Laboratories sold an amphetamine-based inhaler named Benzedrine to treat nasal congestion. In 1937, doctors found they could use amphetamines to improve concentration and performance in people with ADHD.

THE NAME GAME

Drugs are known by many names, and that can be confusing. It can also be dangerous, since some names don't tell you what is really in the drug.

When a drug is first discovered, it is given a chemical name, which describes the molecular structure of the drug. The chemical name is usually too complicated to remember, so a shorter version of the chemical name is developed by researchers to help them talk about the drug.

After the drug has been developed and tested, the **pharmaceutical company** has to get approval to sell the drug. The Food and Drug Administration (FDA) is the US

All drugs should be provided by a licensed doctor or pharmacist.

government agency that makes sure the drug is safe and effective. Once the drug receives FDA approval, it's given two new names. The **generic** (official) name identifies the main ingredient of the drug. The drug is also given a trade or brand name by the company requesting approval for the drug. Only that company can then sell this drug under its brand name for as long as the company has a **patent**, which usually lasts twenty years.

Once the patent expires, other companies may begin to sell the drug under the generic name or their own trade name. The FDA regulates production of both brand-name and generic drugs and the overall quality should be similar.

The generic name amphetamine is a shortened form of its chemical name alpha-methylphenethylamine. Amphetamines are used to make many brand-name drugs, including Adderall. So, someone who takes Adderall is really taking an amphetamine.

Doctors soon started prescribing amphetamines to treat conditions like low blood pressure, sleep disorders, and **depression**, and for weight reduction. Pregnant women were given amphetamines to help reduce nausea. Amphetamines were popular because of their low price and lasting effects. Unfortunately, doctors did not realize at the time that people could get addicted. Synthetic ephedrine was actually sold over the counter (without a doctor's prescription) until 1954.

During the Second World War in the 1940s, many soldiers from the United States, Great Britain, Germany, and Japan took amphetamines to stay awake while on duty as well as to improve their mood and increase their endurance. It was also given to soldiers during the Korean and Vietnam Wars. Even today, amphetamines are sometimes used by the US military, especially by pilots who have to fly long missions.

By the 1950s, the use of amphetamines in the United States was rising. College students, truck drivers, athletes, and others used amphetamines to stay awake, increase endurance, or just boost their confidence. In the 1960s, people started using needles to inject amphetamines for faster and stronger effects, especially people who were already using illegal drugs. By 1962, pharmaceutical companies were producing 80,000 kilograms (176,370 pounds) of amphetamines annually in the United States, according to the FDA. This amounted to forty-three standard **doses** per US citizen per year!

The possession or use of illegal drugs can lead to serious problems, including arrest and jail.

Seeing the Dangers

Studies conducted in the late 1950s and early 1960s began to report that amphetamines could have bad effects on the bodies and minds of people using them. The US government decided to control their use and distribution. By 1959, the FDA had banned amphetamine-based inhalers. In 1965, it became illegal to obtain amphetamines in the United States except by a doctor's prescription.

In 1971, the government moved amphetamines to a higher level of control, called Schedule II status. Schedule II drugs can be used only by prescription and it is against the law to manufacture, distribute, or possess them. Penalties include fines, or imprisonment, or both. The government and schools also made stronger efforts to educate the public about the danger of amphetamines.

Despite these steps, the use of amphetamines began rising again in the 1980s. Part of this was caused by people who made the drug in secret, illegal labs. To help stop the growth, the federal government regulated the chemicals that people use to produce illegal amphetamines. That helped at first, but then US companies began having problems obtaining the chemicals they needed for legal production. Foreign companies now provide much of the US supply, and the government has had trouble controlling the flow of these chemicals from other countries.

Amphetamine abuse continues to be a major problem, hurting the lives of kids and teens as well as adults.

CHAPTER TWO

Dangerous Substitute

POP MUSIC SUPERSTAR FERGIE IS WORLD famous. She's a singer, songwriter, and member of the music group The Black Eyed Peas. She has toured the world, performed at the Super Bowl, sold millions of records, and won several Grammy awards.

On her way to a successful career, however, Fergie faced many difficulties. Perhaps the worst one was her addiction to crystal meth, a particularly strong and dangerous drug in the amphetamine family.

Fergie started her career as a child, performing in commercials and on TV, including the Disney Channel. In the 1990s, Fergie formed the pop group Wild Orchid with two friends. While their first album was a success, their second record did not do as well. With her musical career failing to take off, Fergie began using drugs to feel better. She eventually developed an addiction to crystal methamphetamine, a very powerful amphetamine commonly known as crystal meth.

In an interview with talk show host Oprah Winfrey in 2012, Fergie opened up about her drug history and her struggle with addiction. She said she started using drugs while trying to cope with the stress of fame and trying to maintain her personal identity. She said that, during her time as a member of the group Wild Orchid, she felt completely "inauthentic." She was thinking about leaving the group to go off on her own, but she kept her feelings hidden because she did not want to disappoint her fellow group members. Instead of facing her feelings, she started hanging around with people who were bad influences. She began using Ecstasy, another powerful psychoactive drug, and then moved on to crystal meth.

After using crystal meth for a year, Fergie told Oprah, "I started getting really **paranoid**." She said she believed the FBI (Federal Bureau of Investigation) was following her. One day she went into a church to hide from the police, whom she was convinced were after her. While waiting inside the church in fear, she made a vow to her "higher power" that, if there was no SWAT team waiting for her when she went outside, she would get off the drugs. Sure enough, no police were outside when she left the church. Fergie told Oprah that was the day she decided to stop taking drugs for good. She said that her recovery included "a lot of **therapy**, soul searching, and discovering why I did the drugs in the first place."

Pop superstar Fergie shared her story about drug addiction and recovery with Oprah Winfrey.

Famous Amphetamine Abusers

Some famous and infamous people have used amphetamines during the height of their careers. Here's a short list.

Adolf Hitler: According to a 2013 National Geographic Channel documentary, Nazi leader Adolf Hitler consumed a daily cocktail of drugs including amphetamines. Professor of Psychiatry and Pharmacology Nassir Ghaemi said that drug use helps explain Hitler's increasingly erratic behavior and paranoia as World War II progressed.

US President John F. Kennedy: President Kennedy had suffered many health problems since childhood and received many different medications over the years. Reports from many sources confirm that Dr. Max Jacobson, known as Dr. Feelgood, administered high-dosage amphetamine shots to President Kennedy on a regular basis.

Judy Garland: Perhaps most famous for starring in the movie *The Wizard of Oz*, Judy Garland was a singer and actress who died from a drug **overdose** in 1969, just weeks after she celebrated her forty-seventh birthday. Early in her life, the pressures of Hollywood took their toll. While still in her teens, Garland was given amphetamines in order to combat her fatigue on movie sets and to control her weight. She went into a downward spiral that resulted in her lifelong drug addiction.

Elvis Presley: Called "the King of Rock 'n' Roll," Presley was introduced to amphetamines by one of his commanding sergeants after being drafted into the army. He continued to use prescription drugs the rest of his life to elevate his mood and combat his feelings of loneliness. Since doctors prescribed his medication, it was much easier for him to hide it from the public. When Presley died, his death report said he had fourteen different prescription medications present within his body. He was only forty-two years old.

Teenager Judy Garland starred in *The Wizard of Oz*.

Fergie eventually kicked her drug habit in 2002. In an interview with *Time* magazine, Fergie said that crystal meth "was the hardest boyfriend I ever had to break up with."

Fergie has now reached a new level of stardom. In January 2015, she told the British newspaper the *Guardian* that it is "imperative" for people with addiction issues to find something to fulfill them. "Absolutely. You have to," she answered when asked if it was important to find another outlet. "For me it was making music and getting my thoughts out."

Many famous people have become addicted to amphetamines, often using them in combination with other drugs. They include actors, musicians, athletes, scientists, and even world leaders. While the drug may make them feel good or perform better at first, their addiction can lead to destructive behavior. That can include poor health, financial and legal problems, and even death.

Amphetamines are a group of synthetic stimulants that are chemically similar to adrenaline, a substance we produce naturally in our bodies. Adrenaline causes a person to feel a strong emotion such as excitement, fear, or anger. In many ways, amphetamines affect the body like adrenaline does, by working on the body's central nervous system and increasing its activity.

There are three main types of amphetamines: amphetamine sulfate, more commonly known as "speed" (also known by its trade name, Benzedrine); dextroamphetamine (Dexedrine or "Dexy's Midnight Runners"); and methamphetamine (Methedrine or "meth"), the most powerful of the three.

Amphetamines stimulate our central nervous system (our nerves and our brains) by increasing the amount of certain chemicals. Our central nervous system is in charge of sending messages all over our body, using nerve cells called neurons. When drugs "kick-start" our nervous system, some of our mental or physical functions may improve for a period of time. Amphetamines also reduce our appetite.

Scientists think amphetamines make our bodies produce more of a substance called dopamine. Dopamine

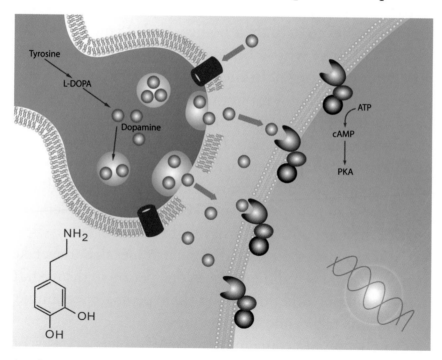

Amphetamines cause the brain to produce more dopamine, a chemical that helps control mood and appetite.

is a neurotransmitter, a brain chemical that communicates information throughout our bodies. The brain uses neurotransmitters to tell your heart to beat, your lungs to breathe, and your stomach to digest. Dopamine helps our brains to produce feelings like pleasure and reward. Dopamine also helps control our movements and our emotions. It helps us to decide what we want and then take action to get it.

When people's bodies produce the right amount of dopamine, they can react normally to the different things they face in life. For people who can't produce enough dopamine on their own, doctors may prescribe drugs like amphetamines to help their bodies produce more.

For children whose brains don't function normally, amphetamines can help them focus their thoughts and concentrate better. Amphetamines can open breathing passages for people with asthma, a lung disease that makes it difficult to get enough air. Their ability to increase energy and alertness helps treat narcolepsy, a rare disease with which people feel an uncontrollable urge to sleep all the time. They can help people with severe weight problems to control their appetite and lose weight.

The amount of prescribed amphetamines that users take each day can be very different from one person to the next. It depends, among other things, on the type of amphetamine, the way it is taken, and the person.

Amphetamines come in the form of tablets, crystals, or powder. They are very often mixed with other substances, and they can be swallowed, snorted, or even smoked.

A Strong Temptation

Problems start when people who don't need a prescription decide to use amphetamines anyway because they think the drugs will help improve something in their lives. They may hear that amphetamines make you feel happier or help you to lose weight. Maybe students want to concentrate better to get higher marks at school. Athletes might want to feel more powerful or ready to compete. People who are shy and feel out of place at parties may want to be more confident and outgoing. Kids may also see their friends using drugs and want to be part of the group and feel like they belong.

In 2014, Cable News Network (CNN) reported that prescription drugs like amphetamines were becoming more and more popular with college students who were

Some youths think amphetamines will help them be more popular, but drug abuse can make them feel even more alone.

looking for a quick fix to help them buckle down and power through their workloads. During the report, Sean McCabe, a professor at the University of Michigan Substance Abuse Research Center, said "Our biggest concern … is the increase we have observed in this behavior over the past decade." According to the report, more than 90 percent of users said they used amphetamines to help them concentrate while studying.

"It helps me stay focused and be more efficient, which is very helpful with the chaos of college," according to one university student who said she takes amphetamine-based Adderall anywhere from once a month to a few times a week, depending on her schedule and workload. Another student said that, after taking Adderall, "I just feel very alive and awake and ready for challenges that come my way." However, neither student wanted to be identified because they were using these prescription drugs illegally.

Researchers believe that it's hard to change these attitudes because many students think "the end justifies the means" and that illegal use of amphetamines was either not dangerous at all or only slightly dangerous.

These students could not be more wrong. "College students tend to underestimate the potential harms associated with the nonmedical use of prescription stimulants," according to Dr. McCabe. Students who abuse amphetamines can ruin their lives.

CHAPTER THREE

A Life Ended Too Soon

FOR KYLE CRAIG, A MUSICIAN, ATHLETE, and student who got good grades at Vanderbilt University, death came suddenly and shockingly.

According to ABC News, Kyle's family called him "strong, large, and in charge," but in just one year, Kyle lost his social confidence and became increasingly paranoid. As his life spiraled downward, hardly anyone noticed. In May 2010, Kyle stepped out in front of a speeding passenger train and ended his life. He was twenty-one years old.

Kyle had been using Adderall, an amphetamine-based medication often prescribed for ADHD. Kyle did not have ADHD, but he wanted something to help him stay up all night during the school year so he could study and perform the next day. By the weekend he would be tired, so he would take more Adderall to build up his energy and go out with his friends. Even worse, he'd often mix the drug with alcohol.

At first, Kyle bought the blue $10 Adderall pills from friends. Later, he pretended he had ADHD and received his own prescription from a doctor. When he came home to visit, his parents started to notice that his personality was changing, but they thought he was just adjusting to college. They didn't realize until it was too late that Kyle was showing dangerous, early-warning signs of psychosis caused by Adderall abuse.

Kyle's mother said, "We feel the loss every minute of every day. We were a family of five, and now we are a family of four." After his death, Kyle's classmates and friends told his parents, "Everyone takes Adderall."

Amphetamine abuse can lead to sadness, depression, and even thoughts of suicide.

People may be pressured to use amphetamines by dealers who make money by trying to get them addicted.

28

As you've already read, amphetamines are commonly prescribed by doctors for many legitimate uses. Unfortunately, their popularity also makes them prime candidates for misuse.

People take amphetamines without a prescription for a variety of reasons. Some start using drugs as part of approved medical treatment but find it hard to stop when their treatment ends. Others use them to help relieve the stress that they feel in their lives, or to improve their performance in school or sports. Still others simply use drugs because their friends do.

According to the Centers for Disease Control and Prevention (CDC), one in twelve Americans is now diagnosed with ADHD. Sales of Adderall and similar drugs have soared more than thirty times since 2001, says the CDC, and so has abuse of the drug.

An estimated one in five students has abused Adderall. According to a 2006 study by the Partnership for a Drug-Free America, usage starts in high school, where one in ten students in grades seven to twelve has used Adderall to help with school performance. They share it, buy it from one another, or fake ADHD to obtain it. The misuse carries on into college, where academic pressures are even greater.

While these students may believe the drug is harmless, the facts prove otherwise. Adderall is a powerful combination of four time-released amphetamines. Fallon Schultz, an addiction specialist from Howell, NJ, said that misuse of the drug may chemically alter the brain. Studies at the

University of California, Los Angeles show that those who use amphetamines have higher rates of aggression, psychosis, and suicide, according to Schultz.

A 2009 report in *Scientific American* magazine suggested that, despite the short-term benefits of the drug, long-term use could change brain function enough to depress mood and boost anxiety. The brains of young students are especially vulnerable because they are not fully developed. Full development isn't achieved until someone reaches his or her mid-twenties.

It doesn't matter if you want to take amphetamines to wake up in the morning, to stay up late studying, or just to have fun. Abusing amphetamines is always dangerous. When amphetamines give you that extra kick of energy, you may feel on top of the world for a brief moment. But when the drugs wear off, there is a terrible crash, which is a good description for how your body feels afterwards. Short-term users may have slight symptoms that last for days, while chronic (long-term) users may experience severe symptoms that can persist for several months.

After the Thrill

When amphetamines wear off, at first you may feel sluggish and disconnected. Since your body's normal functions have been disrupted, you may have trouble falling asleep at night (insomnia) or find it difficult to wake up in the morning.

Many amphetamine users say they feel nervous, jittery, or irritable. Their mouths become unusually dry, and they

have trouble swallowing. Many lose their appetite. Some people get dizzy or have blurred vision. As their energy fades, some people get depressed and confused. Some even experience hallucinations. Others say they experience even worse effects.

Aside from crashing when the drug wears off, amphetamine users feel bodily effects in ways that may not have anything to do with the reason the person is taking them. These are called **side effects**, and some of them can be very dangerous. Side effects can change our bodies or behavior. They can last for a long time, or even be permanent.

For example, amphetamines make the heart beat faster, and they raise blood pressure. They can constrict (shrink or compress) blood vessels and increase blood glucose (the levels of sugar in the blood). They can cause an allergic reaction that includes facial swelling, rashes, and difficulty breathing. Long-term use of amphetamines can cause liver damage or failure, which could require a transplant. In severe cases, amphetamine overdoses can damage the heart and the small blood vessels in the brain, leading to stroke and physical collapse.

When people crash after the amphetamines wear off, their bad feelings usually lead to more **cravings** for the drug. They think that, by taking more amphetamines, the unpleasantness will go away for a while. These cravings can be very powerful because amphetamines are psychostimulants, which means that they can cause both your mind and your body to want to take the drug again once its effects wear off.

Pictures taken before and after Jamie Lynn France's arrest show the heavy price of drug addiction.

For some people, the cravings get so strong that they become addicts, meaning they can't stop using the drug once they get used to it. Continued and extended binges of amphetamine abuse create the most serious effects on the body.

A heavy amphetamine user will waste away physically and become malnourished if these binges are repeated. He or she is likely to look gaunt and unhealthy. This was what happened to Miss Teen Oregon-World beauty queen Jamie Lynn France, who was arrested in Oregon in November 2014 and charged with possession of methamphetamine and other drugs. Officials paired France's mug shot with photos from her reign as a beauty queen to show the public

how drug abuse can change a person's appearance, and to warn them of the dangers of drugs.

Personality can change, and the person might show signs of mental disease, including aggressive, paranoid hostility. There is even a form of psychosis that can occur as an effect of extended amphetamine abuse. Some people suffer from hallucinations that could prompt dangerously violent behavior.

While the person is using amphetamines, he or she is likely to be unaware of the serious effects of the drug. But if that person tries to stop, he or she is going to find out how much they have become **dependent** on the drug.

A Dangerous Gateway

Using amphetamines can lead a person to try other drugs. For this reason, amphetamines are called **gateway drugs**.

Oftentimes, sedatives (sleeping pills) and amphetamines are taken together. While amphetamines help wake you up and make you more alert, abusers may find it hard to sleep afterwards. They then take sedatives to help relax and make it easier to fall asleep. Some people get caught in a cycle of using both amphetamines and sedatives together, trying to use one to counter the effects of the other. This roller-coaster effect is very damaging to the body.

The effects that amphetamines have on our bodies can also decrease over time. This is called tolerance. When that happens, people may have to take stronger doses to get the same result. Sometimes the desire to maintain or heighten

CRYSTAL METH KILLS

Crystal meth is short for crystal methamphetamine, one form of the drug methamphetamine.

Crystal meth is abused by individuals of all ages, but is most commonly used as a "club drug," taken while partying. Its most common street names are ice or glass.

People take crystal meth by snorting it (inhaling through the nose), smoking it, injecting it with a needle, or even by mouth. From the start, crystal meth begins to destroy the user's life.

Crystal meth burns up the body's resources, creating a devastating dependence that can only be relieved by taking more of the drug. Crystal meth's effects are highly concentrated, and many users report getting hooked (addicted) from the first time they use it.

"I tried it once and BOOM! I was addicted," said one meth addict who lost his family, friends, and his profession as a musician, and ended up homeless.

Consequently, it is one of the hardest drug addictions to treat, and many die in its grip.

the effects of amphetamines drives a person to try other, more powerful drugs like cocaine or crystal meth. These substances are even more dangerous and addictive than amphetamines.

People can get so hopeless after dealing with amphetamine abuse that they think about killing themselves. That may have been what happened to Kyle Craig.

The Myth of Better Marks

Some students think taking stimulants without a prescription can mean more As on their report cards. But do these medications really make you a better student?

Definitely not.

The National Institute on Drug Abuse reported in 2014 that ADHD drugs like Adderall do not improve academic performance in teens who don't have ADHD. In fact, the average person who abuses prescription stimulants typically receives lower grades than those who don't abuse these drugs. These students are also more likely than other students to drink alcohol heavily and use other illicit drugs.

CHAPTER FOUR

A Player's Apology

IN DECEMBER 4, 2014, THE NATIONAL
Football League (NFL) made an announcement that
saddened many football fans in Baltimore. On that day, the
league suspended star Baltimore Ravens defensive tackle
Haloti Ngata for the final four games of the regular season
for violating the league's policy on performance-enhancing
substances. Ngata was found to have taken Adderall, an
amphetamine-based drug that helps improve energy
and focus.

In his ninth season, Ngata was having one of his better
years in recent memory. He was helping his team fight for
a playoff spot and a chance to go to the Super Bowl. Now
his team would have to play their most important games
of the season without him.

"I made a mistake, and I own this," Ngata said in a
statement. "I took Adderall and take full responsibility for

Haloti Ngata was suspended for the final four games of the National Football League season in 2014 for using amphetamines.

doing this. I am deeply sorry and broken up over this. I let down my family, my teammates, Ravens fans, and myself."

"This is disappointing news for the Ravens," general manager Ozzie Newsome said. "We are disappointed with Haloti, but no more than he is with himself."

"I was very shocked," said rookie defensive tackle Timmy Jernigan, who replaced Ngata in the starting lineup. "It just didn't sound like Haloti." Luckily for the Ravens, they won three out of their last four games without Ngata to reach the playoffs.

Ngata said he took the drug because the demands of the game and family life—he has three small children—were making him feel sluggish. He wanted to improve his energy and concentration. The toughest part of the suspension, he said, was the feeling that he let his teammates and his family down. He said they bore the burden as well. Ngata, a five-time Pro Bowl defender, lost $2.1 million in salary as a result of the suspension. And after the season, he was traded by the Ravens.

Unfortunately, Ngata's case was not unusual. By the beginning of the 2014 season the NFL had already suspended more than twenty-five players for using banned substances, including stimulants like amphetamines. Football players were not the only professional athletes to be caught using amphetamines and other drugs.

Other professional sports leagues, including Major League Baseball (MLB), the National Basketball Association (NBA), and the National Hockey League (NHL), have been forced

to face the fact that more players are using banned substances to try and gain an advantage over their opponents. The leagues have instituted new testing policies and increased penalties for players who use drugs without prescriptions. The teams know how dangerous these drugs can be, and they want to make sure that players compete fairly.

The sport of cycling has long been tainted by the use of performance-enhancing drugs. One of the most infamous cases of a cyclist misusing amphetamines occurred in July 1967. British cyclist Tommy Simpson was battling diarrhea and had taken an amphetamine and consumed alcohol. Both of these are diuretics, meaning they cause the user to urinate more and reduce the amount of liquid in their bodies. Simpson died of exhaustion during the Tour de France while attempting a climb of Mont Ventoux on a hot day.

British cyclist Tommy Simpson died while racing in the Tour de France after he mixed amphetamines with alcohol.

The problem of amphetamine-based drug abuse in sports is only the tip of the iceberg. Many people today, including students, use amphetamines even though they are not sick.

Kids today feel pressure to succeed at everything they do. They see prescription drugs advertised on TV and other media, and the commercials seem to say that these substances can solve everyone's problems and make life better. Since doctors recommend them, many kids come to believe that these drugs must be safe, even without a doctor's supervision. They also hear that their friends are already using amphetamines, and they don't want to be left behind.

Abusing amphetamines can be very dangerous to a student's health and even their life. When doctors prescribe stimulants, they make their decisions based on the medical condition of the patient. They take into account the person's size, weight, and health. Doctors also consider what amount of the drug should be taken and in what form. They know whether the person has used it before and whether other drugs are going to be taken at the same time.

During treatment, the doctor monitors the person to make sure the drug is working like it should and that there are no unexpected side effects. None of these controls are in place when a person decides to take amphetamines on their own.

Hidden Dangers

People who use amphetamines illegally also can't be sure where their drugs are coming from, or what is in them.

Illegal amphetamines are often stolen or acquired through scams involving pharmacists or physicians who are tricked into writing prescriptions for the drugs. These illegally acquired drugs are then either sold as is or reduced to powder or yellowish crystals that can be ingested in a number of ways, including sniffing and by injection. During this process the seller may mix in other substances. The user has no way of really knowing what they are taking.

There are no controls on the quality, strength, or ingredients of amphetamines made in illegal labs, making them even more dangerous.

DIFFERENT LOOKS

Amphetamines can be found in different forms, from powder to tablets and capsules. They can be wrapped in aluminum foil or packed into plastic bags and even small balloons when sold illegally.

Amphetamine powder can range in color from white to brown, sometimes with traces of pink or gray. It has a strong smell and tastes very bitter if not mixed with something to improve the flavor and odor.

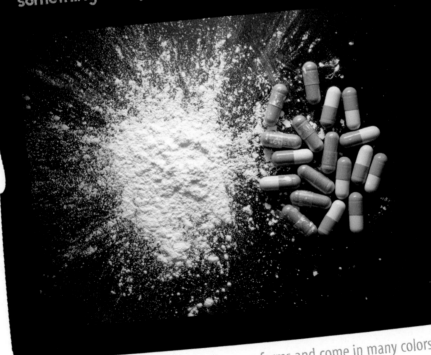

Amphetamines can be used in many forms and come in many colors.

Pills are usually swallowed, but amphetamines can also be smoked, injected directly into the body with a needle, or snorted through the nose.

Amphetamines that are produced illegally can contain other ingredients, some of which can be very harmful on their own. They can include a collection of binding agents (materials that hold the mixture together), caffeine, or sugar. Other drugs may also be added to make the mix even more powerful and dangerous. In reality, the user never knows what they are consuming.

Another means of illegal sale of amphetamines involves look-alike drugs produced in illicit laboratories. Since there are no controls, one batch might be much stronger than another. A person accustomed to using a weak look-alike may unwittingly suffer an overdose taking the same amount of a stronger look-alike.

Bad Behavior

The effects of amphetamines may be felt immediately (if injected or smoked) or within a half-hour (if swallowed or snorted). No matter how illegal amphetamines are consumed, they are likely to change the person's life in a very bad way.

For many, amphetamine abuse controls the way they live their lives. All they can think about is how they can get their next supply. Abusing the drug can lead to **delusions**, hallucinations, and a feeling of paranoia. These feelings can cause a person to act in a bizarre fashion, becoming unusually aggressive and even violent. As their personality changes, they often push away their family and friends while spending more time with their drug supplier and other people who also use the drug.

A Heavy Cost

Beyond losing friends and changing their personality, amphetamine abusers face other big problems.

Students who misuse amphetamines don't perform as well, and they miss class more frequently. They also drop out of school more often. Workers are less productive, and they lose out on promotions and higher pay. Over a lifetime, the losses can add up to tens or hundreds of thousands of dollars.

Students may also not realize at first that using illegal drugs and being treated for addiction costs a lot of money. Regular doctor's appointments for faked amphetamine prescriptions can add up, and street costs are much more expensive. Drug users can easily spend more than half of their available income supporting their habits.

They also experience more health problems, meaning that they spend more on medical bills and health insurance. Because they get in more car accidents and get pulled over more often for things like driving under the influence, their

car insurance costs can rise more than 300 percent, and they can even have their policies canceled.

Addiction hurts people with low income the most. People with less money have tighter budgets and less cash to spare. If a parent gets addicted, his or her children can be trapped in a cycle of poverty for the rest of their lives. Many children of substance abusers also wind up copying their parents' behavior and becoming addicts themselves. This is particularly true for poorer families, where children do not have as much access to better schools or services that can help them learn how to live in a better way.

Breaking the Law

While students may not always understand that they risk their health using amphetamines, many pay even less attention to the fact that non-prescription use is against the law.

"The fact that it's illegal really doesn't cross my mind," one student says. "It's not something that I get nervous about because it's so widespread and simple."

Teens who use amphetamines without a prescription are breaking the law and can end up in court.

In reality, getting caught for using amphetamines illegally can be very serious. The penalty for a first offense of possessing amphetamines without a doctor's prescription can start at a $1,000 fine or a year in prison, or both. If you get caught again, the penalties increase. The punishment for selling or giving away amphetamines is even more severe.

Society Pays

Amphetamine abuse doesn't hurt only the person taking the drug. Society also pays a heavy price.

Using illegal drugs makes workers less productive at their jobs, making their companies less profitable. Drug abusers tend to have more health problems and need more treatment, but they often can't pay for medical care on their own. That means they depend on government health services and treatment centers for help.

Illegal drug use also leads to higher crime rates. Police spend more money to enforce the laws, which also leads to higher costs for drug-related trials and for the housing of drug offenders in jails and prisons.

The National Institute on Drug Abuse (NIDA) and the Surgeon General's office try to estimate the costs to society for substance abuse and addiction. While it is not possible to separate the costs of amphetamine abuse from other drugs, a 2014 report estimates that illegal drug use as a whole costs society about $193 billion each year. That's more than $600 for each person in the United States!

CHAPTER FIVE

Breaking the Chain

IN SPITE OF THE DANGERS, MANY ADULTS and young adults are still tempted to use amphetamines for the reasons already mentioned. Unfortunately, some become dependent on the drug's effects and find they can't stop. They're hooked!

The good news is that help is available. It's not easy by any means, but amphetamine abusers can stop using these drugs, especially if they get help and support from their family and friends.

For someone who wants to stop using amphetamines, the first step is to admit that they have a problem in the first place. With long-term use, amphetamine addiction signs are hard to miss. Here are some questions that students can ask themselves to see if they are addicted:

Signs of amphetamine abuse include a thin or weak appearance and a loss of appetite.

Do I depend on amphetamines? If you started using amphetamines to feel "better" but now take them to just feel "normal," you're probably addicted. According to the National Institute of Drug Abuse, the body becomes dependent on amphetamines over time and can't function normally without them.

Do I have trouble handling my life without amphetamines? Of all the addiction signs, feeling like you need the drug's effects to face the day demonstrates psychological as well as physical dependence. At this point, a person has rearranged his or her entire lifestyle around using amphetamines and looking for the next supply.

Am I taking larger and larger doses? Amphetamines weaken your ability to produce dopamine, so users find themselves taking larger and larger amounts to get the same effects.

Did I try to stop, but couldn't? It gets harder to stop using amphetamines as your body and mind become more dependent on them. When people do try to stop, they often suffer from the effects of withdrawal. Many people can't give up amphetamines without professional treatment.

Do I lose control of my emotions? Amphetamines throw off the balance of chemicals in your brain that control emotions and impulses. Abusing amphetamines for weeks or months can cause unstable behavior, mood swings, and even violence.

Coping with the Comedown

When people first stop using amphetamines, their bodies react in many different ways, most of them bad. For a short time, they may have to feel worse in order to feel better.

Think of it this way. When someone breaks a bone in his or her arm, doctors place the arm in a cast for several weeks to let the bone heal. During that time the muscles in the arm get weak because they haven't been used as much. After the bone heals and the cast comes off, the person needs to exercise to get strength back in the arm muscles.

The body has to heal from drug abuse in much the same way. Your body produces certain chemicals naturally, and these chemicals regulate how you feel. When you take amphetamines, the drug changes the way your body makes these chemicals. The first effects may make some feelings even stronger. You may feel more energetic or alert. However, when you keep taking amphetamines, they begin to hurt your body's ability to produce these substances on its own. You become dependent on using more and more of the drug to get the same effect, or even just to feel normal.

When you finally stop taking amphetamines, your body needs some time to adjust and heal. Your body has gotten used to letting amphetamines create energy and focus instead of doing it naturally. Now your body needs to take some time to remember how to do it without the drug.

Withdrawal is a process during which the body readjusts after depending on amphetamines. During withdrawal you may feel tired instead of energetic and confused instead of

50

Amphetamine withdrawal can be difficult and will take time, but eventually the addict will feel better than when he or she was on the drug.

Narcotics Anonymous and other organizations help teen drug abusers share their experiences with others who understand what they are going through.

alert. You might get irritable and depressed. You may want to sleep a lot. Your stomach may hurt, and your moods may change quickly. Your body will still crave the drug, and you'll be tempted to go back to using amphetamines.

The amount of time that withdrawal takes depends on the amount of amphetamines you've been using and for how long. Withdrawal may last anywhere from a few days to a few weeks. Getting enough sleep and rest to build up your energy can be one of the most important treatment factors to support amphetamine withdrawal.

Getting Help

While some people can break their habit on their own, others may need outside help to make sure they can safely quit. Talking with counselors can help people figure out why they started using amphetamines in the first place and help solve the problems that led to addiction. They can learn ways to avoid amphetamine use and find activities that they enjoy to help them stay away from the drug.

During this time it's very helpful to get support from others who have been amphetamine users because they understand what you are going through. Many recovering teens find it useful to attend meetings at organizations like Narcotics Anonymous, where they can meet and talk with other teens who are going through the same experience. Studies show that teens who attend Narcotics Anonymous meetings are more likely to stay off amphetamines than teens who do not attend meetings.

Know the Warning Signs

If someone you know shows these signs, they could be using amphetamines and need your help to stop:

- Do they look flushed or pale?
- Do they speak very quickly or slur their words?
- Have they lost weight or their appetite?
- Do they look clumsy or uncoordinated?
- Are they having trouble sleeping?
- Do they seem more angry or irritable than usual?
- Do they seem nervous or restless?
- Do you see any skin lesions or blisters?
- Does the person complain about headaches or dizziness?
- Is their behavior erratic, changing quickly from happy and alert to confused and depressed?
- Do they seem to be delusional, seeing or hearing things that don't exist or seeing things that aren't there?

Many recovery programs are also designed to include the friends and family of the recovering amphetamine user. These sessions can help families get back together and repair their relationships.

Some people find it easier to go through amphetamine withdrawal under a doctor's care and even in a hospital. Sometimes doctors slowly remove users from amphetamines, which lessens the effects and lets the body recover over time. In other cases, doctors use medications that may be similar to amphetamines to lessen withdrawal symptoms. Staying in a hospital may help if the person is fighting very strong drug cravings or extreme changes in mood, including anger or even suicidal behavior.

You Can Help

Do you think that you know someone who may be suffering from amphetamine addiction? Would you be able to spot the signs of amphetamine addiction if someone you know were using these drugs?

It's usually hard to notice at first when a person starts using amphetamines. You might just think they're in a good mood or have become more interested in school. However, as the person's use continues to increase, their appearance and behavior change so much that you can start to see warning signs. It's important for you to be able to recognize those signs so you can help someone to stop using the drug.

Here are some questions you can ask yourself to help you decide if someone is abusing amphetamines:

Do you know someone who stays up for days at a time and then sleeps the same way? Trouble sleeping is one of the most common signs of amphetamine addiction. The user may stay awake for a few days while he or she is bingeing on the drug and then, when the crash comes (and it always does come), the user will sleep for two or three days straight, waking only to use the restroom or maybe to get something to drink.

Has someone stopped eating normally? Since amphetamines reduce your appetite, chances are good that the person will skip meals and not eat very much. They may have lost a significant amount of weight. The weight loss will continue as long as amphetamines are being used. As the addiction progresses, the user may care less and less about his or her own health.

Is someone acting strangely or has his or her behavior changed suddenly? The way an amphetamine addict acts can change a lot over time. They can get angry and upset more often and won't appear to be as happy. Sometimes they will act in ways that don't make any sense. One minute they will think they can conquer the world. A short time later they may think that everyone is out to get them. The addiction is tearing the user up inside, causing great harm.

Does someone you know wear long sleeves all the time, even in the summer? If someone hides their arms and legs even in hot weather, there could be a problem with injecting drugs such as amphetamines. Infections often occur as a result of injecting drugs, and they can lead to boils or other

Support from family and friends can help youths break the grip of amphetamine abuse.

serious side effects that create noticeable harm to the skin and other areas of the body. The user may try to cover up these symptoms or otherwise keep the problem out of sight.

Work with Others

At first, people who abuse drugs often deny that they have a problem. If you've confronted someone about his or her amphetamine abuse and the user refuses to admit it, try asking other family members or friends to join together and approach the person as a group. While the person may be angry at first, getting involved could be the way to bring her or him back to health and prevent something even worse from happening. They'll be grateful for the rest of their lives.

Glossary

addictive Something that causes such a strong and harmful need that it becomes difficult to stop.

ADHD (Attention Deficit Hyperactivity Disorder) A condition that makes it hard to pay attention and causes impulsive behavior.

cravings Powerful desires for food, drink, or drugs.

delusions False beliefs that aren't real or backed by the facts.

dependent Relying on drugs or other substances to fulfill a need.

depression A mood disorder that causes strong and lasting feeling of sadness and hopelessness.

dose A quantity of medicine prescribed to be taken at one time.

drug A medicine or other substance that affects the body when taken or used.

gateway drug A drug (such as alcohol, amphetamines, or marijuana) that is thought to lead to the use of more dangerous drugs (such as cocaine or heroin).

generic A drug that is comparable to a brand name drug in strength, purpose, quality, and performance.

overdose The accidental or intentional use of a drug or medicine in a higher amount than is safe.

paranoid Showing a feeling of extreme and irrational fear and distrust about other people and their plans.

patent A government license which gives someone the right to stop others from making, using, or selling an invention or a drug for a set period of time

pharmaceutical company A company that researches, develops, manufactures, and sells drugs for human and animal use.

prescribe To advise and authorize the use of a medicine or treatment; it is usually done in writing.

side effects Any effect of a drug that is different than what was planned, especially if harmful or unpleasant.

stimulant A drug, food, or beverage that quickens or excites the senses.

synthetic Substances produced entirely from chemical reactions in a laboratory.

therapy Treatment intended to cure or alleviate an illness or injury, whether physical or mental.

withdrawal Symptoms that start when the use of a drug ends quickly, many of which may be unpleasant.

Find Out More

Books

Adamec, Christine. *Amphetamines and Methamphetamine.* New York: Facts on File, Inc., 2011.

Killeen, Pam. *Addiction: The Hidden Epidemic: Common Sense Solutions for our #1 Health Problem.* Bloomington, IN: Xlibris Book Publishing, 2010.

Maisto, Stephen, Mark Galizio, and Gerard J. Connors. *Drug Use and Abuse.* Stamford, CT: Cengage Learning, 2015.

Rasmussen, Nicolas. *On Speed: The Many Lives of Amphetamine.* New York: New York University Press, 2009.

Waters, Rosa. *Methamphetamine & Other Amphetamines.* Broomall, PA: Mason Crest, 2014.

Center for Substance Abuse Treatment

www.samhsa.gov/about-us/who-we-are/offices-centers/csat

This website is run by the Substance Abuse and Mental Health Services Administration (SAMHSA). There are links to information about prevention and treatment of drug abuse, and on recovering from drug abuse.

D.A.R.E. America

www.dare.org

D.A.R.E. stands for Drug Abuse Resistance Education. The program is a cooperative effort between community police and schools. There are links to stories of interest for teens on topics such as drug abuse and bullying.

KidsHealth

kidshealth.org

Click on separate links for kids, teens, or parents to get information on many health topics, including drug use.

NIDA For Teens

teens.drugabuse.gov/drug-facts/prescription-stimulant-medications-amphetamines

The NIDA for Teens website was created for middle and high school students and their teachers.

Index

Page numbers in **boldface** are illustrations. Entries in **boldface** are glossary terms.

About the Author

Gerry Boehme is a published author and editor, a business consultant, and a guest speaker at conferences across the United States and around the world. A graduate of the Newhouse School at Syracuse University, he lives on Long Island, New York, with his wife and two children.